Your Life Sucks but I'm so Cute. Copyright © 2024 by Kitty Books

ISBN: 978-91-89848-92-4

All Rights Reserved. No part of this work may be reproduced, incorporated into a computer system, or transmitted in any form or by any means (electronic, mechanical, photocopying, recording or otherwise) without the prior written permission of the copyright holders. Infringement of such rights may constitute an intellectual property crime.

Your life sucks
but I'm so cute

by Kitty Books

Keep moving forward. Or don't. Either way, life goes on without you.

You've got this! And by 'this,' I mean an overwhelming sense of dread.

Don't worry about the future. It's going to be just as disappointing as the present.

Chase your dreams, but don't be surprised if they're running away from you.

Every journey begins with a single step—and an immediate desire to quit.

You're stronger than you think, but weaker than you hoped.

Just because you're struggling doesn't mean you're not failing.

Follow your passion, unless it's napping. Then maybe diversify.

Keep going. You're almost at the point where you'll want to give up.

You can do anything you set your mind to —unless it requires talent or effort.

Every mistake is a lesson. You're basically a professor now.

Today is a new day... to mess things up all over again.

Believe in yourself, even if the evidence strongly suggests you shouldn't.

Take it one day at a time. Honestly, even that might be too ambitious.

Success is around the corner. So, naturally, you took a different street.

Be yourself! Unless 'yourself' is what got you into this mess.

Take a deep breath—because that's all you'll achieve today.

Life's too short to care about what others think, but long enough to second-guess it later.

You've survived 100% of your bad days. Not gracefully, but still.

Your best days are ahead of you... if you stop hitting snooze.

Confidence is key. Too bad you left it in your other pants.

Aim high, but bring a parachute. Statistically, you'll need it.

Keep reaching for the stars—eventually, gravity will remind you who's boss.

You are capable of amazing things, like messing up repeatedly.

Self-care is important; that's why you're procrastinating in style.

Stay humble. It's not like you have another option.

You're one in a million, which technically still makes you replaceable.

Don't let your dreams stay dreams. Let them haunt you at 3 a.m. instead.

Every day is a blank page—except yours is full of coffee stains and doodles.

Happiness is a journey, but your GPS is recalculating.

You're the protagonist of your story, but the supporting cast is stealing the show.

Hard work pays off eventually, but Netflix pays off right now.

Don't let anyone dim your sparkle. You're doing a fine job of that yourself.

The early bird gets the worm, but the snoozing bird avoids unnecessary drama.

Start small. No, smaller. Okay, maybe just think about starting.

You're the total package—just wrapped in several layers of confusion.

Life's a dance, but you're stuck doing the Macarena at a wedding.

Great things take time, which explains why you're still waiting.

Don't be afraid to fall; just make it look intentional.

Don't sweat the small stuff. Focus on the big, terrifying stuff instead.

The glass isn't half full or half empty—it's just dirty and forgotten in the sink.

www.ingramcontent.com/pod-product-compliance
Lightning Source LLC
LaVergne TN
LVHW061632070526
838199LV00071B/6653